# Principles of Value-Centric Management

# (VCM P.I.P.E™)

*A framework for Managing & Leading People from a Value-Centric POV*

**HENDRITH**

Principles of Value-Centric Management (VCM P.I.P.E™): A framework for Managing & Leading People from a Value-Centric POV

© 2024 Hendrith Vanlon Smith Jr . All rights reserved.

No portion of this book may be reproduced, stored in a retrieval system or large language model or transmitted in any form or by any means electronical , mechanical, photocopy, recording, scanning, or other- except for brief quotations in critical reviews or articles, without the prior written permission of the author. Alphabet, Inc and its subsidiaries have permission to display a digital sample of this book.

Quotes from this book may be attributed to Hendrith or Hendrith Vanlon Smith Jr

Library of Congress Cataloging-in-Publication Data Smith Jr, Hendrith Vanlon, 1989-

Principles of Value-Centric Management (VCM P.I.P.E™): A framework for managing & leading people from a value-centric POV

/ Hendrith Vanlon Smith Jr

ISBN: 978-1-300-98751-2

# Contents

Introduction ..................................................................... 5
   What is Value ............................................................. 6
Equity in Value-Centric Management: Shared Decision Rights and Responsibilities ................................................. 9
Leadership and Followership in Value-Centric Management (VCM P.I.P.E™) ........................................................ 13
Idea Meritocracy in VCM P.I.P.E™ ................................ 19
Incentives and Disincentives: The Hidden Levers of Behavior . 23
Internal Creative Destruction: Embracing Change for Growth in Value-Centric Management (VCM P.I.P.E™) .................. 27
Individualized Roles: Unleashing Human Potential in Value-Centric Management (VCM P.I.P.E™) ........................... 31
Compensation: Rewarding Value Creation ..................... 35
Collaboration: The Group-Mind Effect in Value-Centric Management (VCM P.I.P.E™) ...................................... 39
Spontaneous Order: The Harmony of Value-Driven Organization in Value-Centric Management (VCM P.I.P.E™) ............. 43
Respect: The Cornerstone of Human Connection in Value-Centric Management (VCM P.I.P.E™) ........................... 47
Justice: The Bedrock of Trust and Fairness in Value-Centric Management (VCM P.I.P.E™) ...................................... 51
Traditions and Rituals: The Glue that Binds People in Value-Centric Management (VCM P.I.P.E™) ........................... 55
Celebration: Fueling the Fire of Achievement in Value-Centric Management (VCM P.I.P.E™) ...................................... 59
Capital Stewardship: Nurturing the Seeds of Prosperity in Value-Centric Management (VCM P.I.P.E™) ........................... 63
Experimentation: Embracing the Unknown in Value-Centric Management (VCM P.I.P.E™) ...................................... 67

Vision: Illuminating the Path Forward in Value-Centric Management (VCM P.I.P.E™) .................................................... 71

Authentic Data Transparency: Illuminating the Path to Collective Intelligence in Value-Centric Management (VCM P.I.P.E™).... 75

Personal Connections and Team Building: Nurturing the Human Element in Value-Centric Management (VCM P.I.P.E™) ......... 79

Customization: Tailoring VCM P.I.P.E™ for Unique Contexts in Value-Centric Management (VCM P.I.P.E™) ........................... 83

Conclusion: Embracing Value-Centric Management (VCM P.I.P.E™) for a Thriving Future ................................................ 87

# Introduction

I created Value-Centric Management (VCM P.I.P.E™), also known as Synergistic Value Centric People Management (SVCPM™), as a comprehensive approach to managing and leading people that prioritizes the creation and exchange of value. It's a flexible framework that can be implemented in various settings, from businesses and classrooms to boardrooms and committees.

At its core, Value-Centric Management (VCM P.I.P.E™), also known as Synergistic Value Centric People Management (SVCPM™), is a revolutionary approach to leading and managing people. It prioritizes the creation and exchange of value within a dynamic ecosystem of interconnected individuals. VCM recognizes that the true power of a group lies in the synergistic relationships between its members. When individuals come together, their combined strengths and skills amplify value creation far beyond what any one person could achieve alone.

This framework shifts the focus away from traditional hierarchies and rigid goals, placing value at the center of all interactions. It does not, however, eliminate hierarchy or goals. It acknowledges that every individual plays a vital role in the value creation process, and it empowers them to contribute their unique talents and perspectives. By fostering a culture of shared beliefs, collaboration, and innovation, VCM unleashes the full potential of the group, leading to increased productivity, effectiveness, and a profound sense of fulfillment for everyone involved.

VCM is more than just a management style; it's a philosophy that transforms organizations into thriving ecosystems. It's about creating an environment where individuals feel valued, respected, and empowered to contribute their best work. When people feel connected to a shared purpose and are recognized for their contributions, they become more engaged, more creative, and more productive. This synergy, in turn, generates a positive ripple effect, enabling the group to contribute more value to the broader community.

In essence, VCM is about harnessing the collective power of the group to achieve extraordinary results. It's about creating a culture where everyone feels invested in the success of the organization and where the total value output is amplified far beyond the sum of its parts.

## What is Value

**Understanding Value**

When I speak of "value," I am referring to an individual's unique capacity to contribute to the betterment of the group. This value can manifest in various forms, including: **skills, expertise, knowledge, experience, intuition, relationships, status, money, etc.**

**The Benefits of Value-Centric Leadership**

Value-centric management can lead to numerous benefits for both individuals and organizations. It can foster a more engaged, motivated, and fulfilled workforce, leading to increased productivity, creativity, and innovation. It can also create a more positive and inclusive organizational culture, where individuals feel valued, respected, and supported. Finally, VCM can contribute to the accomplishment of various success measure – such as profit.

Moreover, value-centric leadership can enhance an organization's reputation and attract top talent. In today's competitive job market, individuals are increasingly seeking out organizations that prioritize employee well-being, personal growth, and a sense of purpose.

**Conclusion**

Value-centric management is not just a management philosophy; it's a commitment to creating a more human-centered and fulfilling organizational experience. It's about recognizing the unique value that each individual brings to the table and empowering them to reach their full potential. By embracing the principles of value-centric leadership, organizations can create a thriving ecosystem where everyone benefits, both individually and collectively.

# Equity in Value-Centric Management: Shared Decision Rights and Responsibilities

In the realm of Value-Centric Management (VCM), the concept of equity takes on a profound significance. It's not just about fairness; it's about recognizing the inherent value and potential within every member of the group. This philosophy extends to decision-making rights and responsibilities, which are not confined to the upper echelons of leadership but are instead distributed throughout the organization.

Imagine a workplace where everyone has a voice, where ideas and insights are welcomed from all corners. This is the essence of VCM's approach to equity. By empowering individuals at all levels to participate in decision-making, it fosters a sense of ownership and responsibility that transcends traditional hierarchical structures.

When people feel that their opinions matter, they become more invested in the group's success. They're no longer just cogs in a machine but active contributors shaping the organization's trajectory. This shared sense of responsibility helps to prevent the "tragedy of the commons," where individuals prioritize their own self-interest at the expense of the collective good.

In a VCM environment, decision-making becomes a collaborative process. It's about harnessing the collective intelligence of the group, recognizing that the best ideas can come from anyone, regardless of their title or position. This approach not only leads to better decisions but also fosters a culture of innovation and continuous improvement.

Moreover, VCM's emphasis on equity promotes transparency and accountability. When everyone has a stake in the decision-making process, there's a greater sense of openness and trust. Resources are managed more sustainably, and individuals are held accountable for their actions.

This approach also has a profound impact on the overall culture of the organization. It encourages collaboration and open communication, as individuals feel empowered to share their ideas and perspectives. It breaks down silos and fosters a sense of unity, as everyone works together towards a common goal.

Ultimately, VCM's focus on equity leads to a more efficient and effective decision-making process. It empowers individuals, fosters collaboration, and creates a more sustainable and accountable environment. It's a philosophy that recognizes the inherent value in every member of the group and harnesses that value to achieve collective success.

By embracing equity in decision-making, organizations can tap into the full potential of their workforce. It's about creating a culture where everyone feels heard, valued, and empowered to contribute their unique talents and perspectives. This not only benefits the individuals within the group but also leads to better outcomes and a more sustainable future for the organization as a whole.

In a world that's becoming increasingly complex and interconnected, VCM's emphasis on equity offers a powerful solution. It's a model for creating organizations that are not only successful but also just, equitable, and sustainable. By putting value at the center of decision-making, VCM paves the way for a brighter future for all.

# Leadership and Followership in Value-Centric Management (VCM P.I.P.E™)

In the realm of Value-Centric Management (VCM P.I.P.E™), leadership takes on a refreshingly inclusive and empowering dimension. It's not about climbing a corporate ladder or attaining a prestigious title; it's about recognizing the inherent potential for leadership within every individual.

At its core, leadership in VCM P.I.P.E™ is about enabling and empowering others to reach their full potential in creating value. It's about recognizing that each person possesses unique strengths and talents, and fostering an environment where those talents can shine. It's about guiding, inspiring, and supporting others to maximize their contributions.

This approach to leadership is crucial because it optimizes the collective output of the group. When individuals are encouraged to lead in their areas of expertise, it creates a powerful synergy where the whole becomes greater than the sum of its parts. It's about tapping into the diverse skill sets within the group and leveraging them to achieve shared goals.

Imagine a musical ensemble. Each musician possesses mastery over their instrument. The conductor might lead the overall performance, but within each section, there are opportunities for leadership. The first violinist might guide the string section, while the lead trumpet player sets the tone for the brass.

Similarly, in a business setting, a software developer might be a technical leader, mentoring their colleagues in coding best practices. A marketing expert might spearhead a campaign strategy, sharing their insights to drive results. Even in a classroom, a student who excels in a particular subject can become a leader, helping their peers grasp challenging concepts.

VCM P.I.P.E™ operates on the premise that everyone has the capacity to excel at something. It's about identifying those areas of strength and encouraging individuals to step up and lead in those domains. This not only boosts individual confidence and fulfillment but also contributes significantly to the overall productivity and success of the group.

When people are given the opportunity to lead in their areas of expertise, they become more engaged and motivated. They feel a sense of ownership and pride in their work, which naturally translates into higher quality output. This, in turn, creates a positive ripple effect, inspiring others to strive for excellence and contribute their own unique talents.

Furthermore, this approach to leadership fosters a culture of collaboration and mutual respect. It dismantles traditional barriers and encourages individuals to learn from each other, regardless of their formal titles or positions. It creates an environment where everyone feels valued and empowered to contribute their best.

This democratization of leadership also enhances adaptability and resilience. In a rapidly changing world, organizations need to be agile and responsive. When leadership is distributed throughout the group, it allows for quicker decision-making and a greater capacity to adapt to new challenges.

Moreover, VCM P.I.P.E™'s leadership philosophy promotes a sense of shared purpose and collective responsibility. It's not just about individual achievement but about contributing to the greater good of the group. This creates a sense of camaraderie and shared ownership, which can be a powerful motivator.

In essence, VCM P.I.P.E™'s philosophy of leadership is about unleashing the full potential of every individual within the group. It's about recognizing that leadership is not a privilege but a responsibility that everyone can and should embrace. By fostering a culture where everyone leads in their own way, VCM P.I.P.E™ creates a dynamic and thriving environment where growth, innovation, and collective success are not just possible but inevitable.

In the symphony of Value-Centric Management (VCM P.I.P.E™), followership plays an equally crucial role as leadership. It's not about blind obedience or passive acceptance; it's about active engagement, critical thinking, and a willingness to support and learn from those who excel in specific areas.

Effective followership is the bedrock upon which successful leadership stands. It's about recognizing that no one person can be an expert in everything. There will always be areas where others possess greater knowledge, skills, or experience. In these instances, embracing followership allows individuals to tap into the expertise of others, accelerating their own growth and contributing to the collective success of the group.

Think of it as a relay race. Each runner has their own leg to complete, and the success of the team depends on each runner performing their part to the best of their ability. The baton pass is a moment of followership, where one runner trusts another to carry the momentum forward. Similarly, in a VCM P.I.P.E™ environment, individuals recognize when it's time to pass the baton, allowing those with greater expertise to lead the way.

Followership is not about relinquishing one's own agency or voice. It's about active participation, asking insightful questions, and providing constructive feedback. A good follower challenges the leader, pushing them to think critically and consider alternative perspectives. This dynamic interplay between leadership and followership creates a fertile ground for innovation and growth.

Moreover, followership is not a static state. It's a fluid and adaptable role that can shift depending on the context. Today's follower might be tomorrow's leader, as individuals develop new skills and expertise. VCM P.I.P.E™ encourages this fluidity, recognizing that everyone has the potential to lead and follow at different times and in different areas.

In essence, followership in VCM P.I.P.E™ is about recognizing and respecting the expertise of others, while also actively contributing one's own unique perspectives and talents. It's about creating a collaborative environment where everyone feels empowered to learn, grow, and contribute to the collective success of the group. By embracing both leadership and followership, individuals and organizations can unlock their full potential and achieve remarkable results.

# Idea Meritocracy in VCM P.I.P.E™

In the dynamic landscape of Value-Centric Management (VCM P.I.P.E™), the principle of Idea Meritocracy stands as a beacon of innovation and progress. It's a philosophy that transcends traditional hierarchies and empowers every individual, regardless of their position or title, to contribute their ideas and insights. In essence, it's about ensuring that the best ideas win, fostering a culture where merit reigns supreme.

**The Essence of Idea Meritocracy**

At its core, Idea Meritocracy is about creating a level playing field for ideas. It's about recognizing that brilliance can emerge from anywhere within an organization, and that the most valuable contributions may not always come from those in positions of authority. This approach challenges the conventional top-down model of decision-making, where ideas are often filtered through layers of hierarchy, potentially stifling creativity and innovation.

In a VCM P.I.P.E™ environment, Idea Meritocracy is not just a buzzword; it's a lived reality. It's about actively seeking out and valuing ideas from all members of the group, regardless of their background or experience. It's about creating a safe space where individuals feel comfortable sharing their thoughts, knowing that their contributions will be judged solely on their merit.

**Benefits of Idea Meritocracy**

The benefits of embracing Idea Meritocracy are manifold. First and foremost, it fosters a culture of innovation. When individuals feel empowered to share their ideas, it sparks a creative energy that can lead to breakthroughs and new solutions. It encourages everyone to think outside the box, challenge assumptions, and explore new possibilities.

Moreover, Idea Meritocracy promotes a sense of ownership and engagement. When people see their ideas being implemented and recognized, it reinforces their sense of value and contribution to the group. This can lead to increased motivation, productivity, and overall job satisfaction.

Furthermore, this approach to decision-making can lead to better outcomes. By considering a wider range of perspectives and ideas, organizations are more likely to identify optimal solutions and avoid potential pitfalls. It's about harnessing the collective intelligence of the group to make informed and effective decisions.

**Implementing Idea Meritocracy**

While the concept of Idea Meritocracy is simple and compelling, its implementation requires a deliberate and sustained effort. It's about creating a culture where ideas are not only welcomed but actively sought out and evaluated. It's about establishing clear channels for communication and feedback, ensuring that everyone has a voice and that their contributions are acknowledged.

Moreover, it's about creating a system for evaluating ideas based on their merit, not on the status or authority of the person presenting them. This requires objective criteria and transparent processes, ensuring that the best ideas rise to the top, regardless of their origin.

**Examples of Idea Meritocracy in Action**

Idea Meritocracy can manifest in various ways within an organization. It could be a suggestion box where employees can submit their ideas, a regular brainstorming session where everyone is encouraged to participate, or even a company-wide hackathon where teams compete to develop innovative solutions.

In a classroom setting, Idea Meritocracy might involve encouraging students to challenge the teacher's ideas or propose alternative approaches. In a community organization, it could mean actively seeking input from residents on how to improve local services or address community challenges.

**Conclusion**

In conclusion, Idea Meritocracy is a cornerstone of Value-Centric Management (VCM P.I.P.E™). It's a philosophy that empowers individuals, fosters innovation, and leads to better decision-making and outcomes. By creating a culture where the best ideas win, regardless of their source, organizations can tap into the full potential of their people and achieve sustainable success. It's about recognizing that everyone has something valuable to contribute, and that the collective intelligence of the group is far greater than the sum of its parts.

# Incentives and Disincentives: The Hidden Levers of Behavior

In the intricate dance of human interaction, incentives and disincentives act as the subtle yet powerful forces that shape behavior. Value-Centric Management (VCM P.I.P.E™) recognizes the profound impact of these forces, both seen and unseen, and emphasizes the importance of aligning them with the group's objectives.

**Incentives: The Power of Positive Reinforcement**

Incentives, whether tangible or intangible, are the rewards that motivate individuals to act in certain ways. They can take many forms, from financial bonuses and promotions to recognition, praise, and opportunities for growth. In a VCM P.I.P.E™ environment, incentives are carefully designed to encourage behaviors that contribute to the creation and exchange of value. And value is defined by the groups goals. Adding value means doing things that enable the group to accomplish its goals.

For instance, a company might implement a profit-sharing program that rewards employees for their collective contributions to the bottom line. This incentivizes collaboration and a focus on overall company success rather than individual gain. Similarly, a school might recognize students not just for academic achievements but also for acts of kindness and community service, fostering a culture of compassion and social responsibility.

However, incentives are not always obvious. They can be embedded in the very fabric of an organization's culture, policies, and procedures. Every rule, every unspoken expectation, every reaction to behavior, carries with it an implicit incentive. It's crucial for leaders to be mindful of these hidden levers and ensure they are aligned with the desired outcomes.

**Disincentives: The Art of Gentle Deterrence**

Just as incentives encourage certain behaviors, disincentives discourage others. They are the consequences, often negative, that deter individuals from engaging in actions that are detrimental to the group's goals. These can range from formal reprimands and penalties to social disapproval and loss of privileges.

For example, a company might implement a policy of progressive discipline for employees who consistently underperform, creating a disincentive for complacency. Similarly, a community might impose fines for littering or vandalism, discouraging behaviors that harm the shared environment.

However, disincentives should be used judiciously and with a focus on rehabilitation rather than punishment. They should be clear, consistent, and proportionate to the offense. Overreliance on disincentives can create a culture of fear and resentment, undermining the trust and collaboration that are essential for a thriving VCM P.I.P.E™ environment.

**The Importance of Alignment**

The key to effectively utilizing incentives and disincentives lies in their alignment with the group's objectives. When these forces are in harmony, they create a powerful momentum that propels the group towards its goals. However, when they are misaligned, they can lead to unintended consequences and counterproductive behaviors.

For instance, if a sales team is incentivized solely based on individual sales volume, it might create a cutthroat environment where collaboration and teamwork suffer. On the other hand, if the incentives are tied to both individual and team performance, it fosters a sense of shared responsibility and encourages cooperation.

**Conclusion**

In the tapestry of VCM P.I.P.E™, incentives and disincentives are the threads that weave together individual actions and collective goals. They are the subtle yet powerful forces that shape behavior, influence decision-making, and ultimately determine the success of the group. By understanding and harnessing these forces, leaders can create an environment where individuals are motivated to contribute their best, fostering a culture of value creation, collaboration, and sustainable growth.

# Internal Creative Destruction: Embracing Change for Growth in Value-Centric Management (VCM P.I.P.E™)

In the dynamic world of Value-Centric Management (VCM P.I.P.E™), the concept of "Internal Creative Destruction" emerges as a powerful catalyst for growth and adaptation. It's a philosophy that recognizes the inevitability of change and encourages organizations to proactively embrace it from within, rather than succumbing to external pressures.

**The Essence of Internal Creative Destruction**

At its core, Internal Creative Destruction is about challenging the status quo and constantly seeking better ways to create and deliver value. It's about recognizing that no process, procedure, rule, or method is sacred. The only constants in a VCM P.I.P.E™ environment are the guiding principles, which provide a stable foundation while everything else is subject to evolution.

This approach acknowledges that clinging to outdated practices or resisting change can be detrimental in the long run. If an organization fails to adapt internally, it risks being disrupted by external forces, potentially leading to obsolescence or even failure. By embracing Internal Creative Destruction, organizations can stay ahead of the curve, continuously innovating and improving to remain competitive and relevant.

**The Role of Leadership**

Leadership plays a crucial role in fostering a culture of Internal Creative Destruction. It's about creating an environment where experimentation and risk-taking are encouraged, and where failure is seen as a learning opportunity rather than a cause for punishment. Leaders must be willing to challenge existing norms, question assumptions, and empower their teams to explore new ideas and approaches.

This doesn't mean abandoning all sense of stability or structure. The guiding principles of VCM P.I.P.E™ provide a framework for decision-making and ensure that change is purposeful and aligned with the organization's values. It's about striking a balance between maintaining a strong foundation and embracing the dynamism necessary for growth.

**Benefits of Internal Creative Destruction**

Embracing Internal Creative Destruction can lead to numerous benefits for organizations. It fosters a culture of continuous improvement, where individuals are constantly seeking ways to enhance efficiency, productivity, and customer satisfaction. It encourages innovation, allowing organizations to develop new products, services, and business models that meet evolving market needs.

Moreover, it enhances adaptability and resilience. In a world of rapid technological advancements and shifting market dynamics, organizations that can quickly pivot and embrace change are more likely to thrive. Internal Creative Destruction builds this capacity for adaptation into the very DNA of the organization.

**Examples of Internal Creative Destruction**

Internal Creative Destruction can manifest in various ways within an organization. It could involve rethinking traditional job roles and responsibilities, adopting new technologies and processes, or even disrupting existing business models to create new sources of value.

For instance, a company might decide to shift from a hierarchical structure to a more agile and self-organizing model, empowering teams to make decisions and take ownership of their work. Or, a retailer might embrace e-commerce and digital marketing, transforming its traditional brick-and-mortar business to meet the demands of the modern consumer.

**Conclusion**

In the ever-evolving landscape of business and society, Internal Creative Destruction is not just an option; it's a necessity. It's about recognizing that change is inevitable and embracing it as an opportunity for growth and transformation. By fostering a culture of innovation, adaptability, and continuous improvement, organizations can navigate the complexities of the modern world and achieve sustainable success. If creative destruction is not allowed to exist within the group, it will in time force its way upon the group from without.

# Individualized Roles: Unleashing Human Potential in Value-Centric Management (VCM P.I.P.E™)

In the realm of Value-Centric Management (VCM P.I.P.E™), the concept of "Individualized Roles" stands as a testament to the philosophy's commitment to recognizing and leveraging the unique talents and capabilities of each person. It's a departure from the traditional one-size-fits-all approach to job descriptions and titles, instead advocating for a more personalized and dynamic approach to role definition.

**The Essence of Individualized Roles**

At its core, Individualized Roles is about aligning an individual's strengths and passions with the needs and objectives of the group. It's about recognizing that each person brings a unique set of skills, experiences, and perspectives to the table, and that these can be harnessed to create greater value for both the individual and the collective.

This approach challenges the conventional practice of creating rigid job descriptions and then seeking individuals to fit those molds. Instead, VCM P.I.P.E™ encourages a more fluid and adaptive approach, where roles are shaped and redefined based on the individual's capabilities and the evolving needs of the organization.

**Benefits of Individualized Roles**

The benefits of embracing Individualized Roles are significant. First and foremost, it leads to increased productivity. When individuals are allowed to focus on tasks that leverage their strengths and passions, they are more likely to be engaged, motivated, and ultimately, more productive. It's about creating an environment where people can do what they do best, leading to higher quality output and greater overall efficiency.

Moreover, Individualized Roles fosters a sense of ownership and fulfillment. When people feel that their roles are tailored to their unique talents and interests, they are more likely to feel valued and appreciated. This can lead to increased job satisfaction, loyalty, and a greater sense of purpose within the organization.

Furthermore, this approach allows organizations to tap into the full potential of their workforce. By recognizing and utilizing the diverse skills and perspectives of their employees, organizations can unlock hidden talents and create a more dynamic and innovative culture.

**Implementing Individualized Roles**

Implementing Individualized Roles requires a shift in mindset and a willingness to embrace flexibility and adaptability. It's about moving away from rigid job descriptions and titles and towards a more collaborative and dynamic approach to role definition.

This involves open communication and ongoing dialogue between individuals and their managers or team leaders. It's about understanding each person's strengths, weaknesses, and aspirations, and finding ways to align those with the needs of the organization. It's also about creating a culture where individuals feel empowered to propose new ideas and take on new challenges, even if they fall outside their traditional job descriptions.

**Examples of Individualized Roles in Action**

Individualized Roles can manifest in various ways within an organization. It could involve allowing employees to take on projects that align with their passions, even if they are outside their formal job responsibilities. It could also mean creating flexible work arrangements that accommodate individual needs and preferences.

For instance, a marketing professional with a passion for graphic design might be given the opportunity to lead the development of visual content for the company's marketing campaigns. Or, a software engineer with a strong interest in user experience might be involved in the design and testing of new product features.

**Conclusion**

In the realm of VCM P.I.P.E™, Individualized Roles is a powerful tool for unleashing human potential and maximizing value creation. It's about recognizing the unique talents and capabilities of each person and creating an environment where those talents can flourish. By embracing flexibility, adaptability, and open communication, organizations can create a more engaged, fulfilled, and productive workforce, ultimately leading to greater success for both individuals and the collective.

# Compensation: Rewarding Value Creation

In the realm of Value-Centric Management (VCM P.I.P.E™), compensation is not merely a transactional exchange for services rendered; it's a strategic tool for recognizing and rewarding the creation of value. This approach challenges traditional compensation models that rely heavily on job titles and hierarchical structures, instead advocating for a system that directly links rewards to the value individuals contribute to the organization.

**The Essence of Value-Based Compensation**

At its core, value-based compensation is about aligning rewards with contributions. It's about recognizing that individuals can create value in various ways, both within and beyond their defined job roles. In a VCM P.I.P.E™ environment, compensation is not solely determined by one's position in the hierarchy but rather by the tangible and intangible value they bring to the table.

This approach acknowledges that traditional compensation models can be limiting and demotivating. When rewards are tied solely to job titles, it can create a sense of stagnation and discourage individuals from going above and beyond their prescribed duties. Value-based compensation, on the other hand, fosters a culture of initiative and innovation, as individuals are incentivized to seek out opportunities to create additional value for the organization.

**Benefits of Value-Based Compensation**

The benefits of adopting a value-based compensation model are numerous. First and foremost, it promotes a sense of fairness and equity. When individuals are rewarded based on their contributions, it creates a meritocratic system where hard work and initiative are recognized and valued. This can lead to increased motivation, engagement, and overall job satisfaction.

Moreover, value-based compensation encourages individuals to think beyond their defined roles and seek out opportunities to create additional value for the organization. This can lead to increased innovation, improved efficiency, and a greater sense of ownership and responsibility among employees.

Furthermore, this approach can help attract and retain top talent. In a competitive job market, organizations that offer a compensation system that rewards value creation are more likely to attract and keep high-performing individuals who are driven by a sense of purpose and impact.

**Implementing Value-Based Compensation**

Implementing a value-based compensation model requires a thoughtful and strategic approach. It's about defining clear metrics for measuring value creation, both in terms of tangible outcomes and intangible contributions. It's also about establishing transparent and objective processes for evaluating and rewarding performance.

This might involve developing new performance metrics that go beyond traditional measures like sales volume or production output. It could also include incorporating peer feedback and 360-degree evaluations to capture a more holistic view of an individual's contributions.

**Conclusion**

In the world of VCM P.I.P.E™, compensation is not just a paycheck; it's a recognition of value creation. By aligning rewards with contributions, organizations can foster a culture of initiative, innovation, and shared success. It's an approach that empowers individuals, promotes fairness, and ultimately drives sustainable growth and prosperity for all.

# Collaboration: The Group-Mind Effect in Value-Centric Management (VCM P.I.P.E™)

In the symphony of Value-Centric Management (VCM P.I.P.E™), collaboration emerges as a harmonious melody, where individual voices blend to create a richer, more powerful sound. It's a philosophy that recognizes the inherent value of collective intelligence, where the sum is truly greater than its parts.

**The Essence of Collaboration**

At its core, collaboration is about harnessing the diverse perspectives, skills, and experiences of individuals within a group to achieve shared goals. It's about creating an environment where open communication, mutual respect, and a willingness to learn from one another are paramount. In a VCM P.I.P.E™ environment, collaboration is not just encouraged; it's woven into the very fabric of the organization's culture.

This approach challenges the traditional notion of competition and individualism, recognizing that true progress often emerges from the cross-pollination of ideas and insights. It's about creating a space where individuals feel empowered to share their knowledge, challenge assumptions, and build upon each other's contributions.

## The Group-Mind Effect

VCM P.I.P.E™ refers to this phenomenon as the "Group-Mind Effect." It's the recognition that when individuals come together in a spirit of collaboration, they create a collective intelligence that surpasses the capabilities of any single person. It's about tapping into the wisdom of the crowd, where diverse perspectives and experiences converge to generate innovative solutions and breakthrough ideas.

This effect is particularly powerful in today's complex and interconnected world. The challenges we face often require multi-faceted solutions that draw upon a wide range of expertise. Collaboration allows us to leverage the collective knowledge and creativity of the group, leading to more effective and sustainable outcomes.

## Benefits of Collaboration

The benefits of collaboration are manifold. It fosters a culture of innovation, as individuals are exposed to new ideas and perspectives, sparking creativity and problem-solving. It enhances decision-making, as a wider range of viewpoints are considered, leading to more informed and balanced choices.

Moreover, collaboration promotes a sense of shared ownership and responsibility. When individuals work together towards a common goal, they develop a sense of camaraderie and mutual support. This can lead to increased motivation, engagement, and a greater sense of purpose within the group.

Furthermore, collaboration can lead to improved efficiency and productivity. By sharing knowledge and resources, individuals can avoid duplication of effort and leverage each other's strengths. This can result in faster project completion times, reduced costs, and a more streamlined workflow.

**Fostering Collaboration**

Creating a collaborative environment requires intentional effort and a commitment to fostering open communication and mutual respect. It's about establishing clear channels for sharing ideas and feedback, and creating opportunities for individuals to connect and interact with one another.

Moreover, it's about recognizing and rewarding collaborative efforts. When individuals see that their contributions to the collective are valued and appreciated, it reinforces the importance of teamwork and encourages continued collaboration.

**Conclusion**

In the tapestry of VCM P.I.P.E™, collaboration is the thread that binds individuals together, creating a vibrant and interconnected network of shared knowledge and purpose. It's a philosophy that recognizes the power of collective intelligence and harnesses it to achieve remarkable results. By fostering a culture of collaboration, organizations can tap into the full potential of their people, driving innovation, enhancing decision-making, and ultimately creating a more fulfilling and prosperous future for all.

# Spontaneous Order: The Harmony of Value-Driven Organization in Value-Centric Management (VCM P.I.P.E™)

In the realm of Value-Centric Management (VCM P.I.P.E™), the concept of "Spontaneous Order" emerges as a guiding principle for creating a harmonious and productive organizational structure. It's a philosophy that recognizes the power of self-organization and the natural emergence of order when individuals are aligned around a shared purpose and a common set of values.

**The Essence of Spontaneous Order**

At its core, Spontaneous Order is about allowing structures and systems to evolve organically, rather than imposing them from the top down. It's about recognizing that individuals, when given the freedom and autonomy to pursue their own value-creating activities, will naturally gravitate towards patterns of cooperation and collaboration that benefit the collective.

This approach challenges the traditional command-and-control model of management, where rigid hierarchies and predefined processes often stifle creativity and innovation. In a VCM

P.I.P.E™ environment, order is not imposed; it's allowed to emerge spontaneously from the interactions and relationships of individuals within the group.

**The Role of Value**

In a VCM P.I.P.E™ context, value acts as the guiding force behind Spontaneous Order. When individuals are aligned around a shared purpose of creating and exchanging value, they naturally seek out opportunities to collaborate and contribute their unique skills and talents. This creates a self-organizing system where individuals find their own place within the group, contributing to the collective good in a way that is both meaningful and fulfilling.

This approach stands in stark contrast to organizational structures that prioritize hierarchy or the status quo. In such systems, order is often maintained through rigid rules and regulations, which can stifle creativity and limit individual autonomy. Spontaneous Order, on the other hand, allows for a more dynamic and adaptable structure that can respond to changing circumstances and evolving needs.

**Benefits of Spontaneous Order**

Embracing Spontaneous Order can lead to numerous benefits for organizations. It fosters a culture of innovation and adaptability, as individuals are empowered to experiment and explore new ideas without fear of reprisal. It promotes a sense of ownership and responsibility, as individuals are encouraged to take initiative and contribute their unique talents to the group.

Moreover, Spontaneous Order can lead to increased efficiency and productivity. When individuals are free to self-organize and collaborate in ways that leverage their strengths, it can lead to more streamlined processes, faster decision-making, and a greater sense of collective purpose.

**Fostering Spontaneous Order**

Creating an environment where Spontaneous Order can flourish requires a commitment to trust, autonomy, and open communication. It's about providing individuals with the freedom to explore their own ideas and initiatives, while also establishing clear guidelines and expectations to ensure alignment with the group's overall goals.

Moreover, it's about cultivating a culture of mutual respect and collaboration, where individuals feel comfortable sharing their perspectives and challenging assumptions. This creates a fertile ground for the emergence of new ideas and innovative solutions.

**Conclusion**

In the symphony of VCM P.I.P.E™, Spontaneous Order is the conductor that allows individual voices to harmonize and create a beautiful and powerful melody. It's a philosophy that recognizes the inherent wisdom and creativity within each person and empowers them to contribute their unique talents to the collective good. By embracing Spontaneous Order, organizations can create a more dynamic, adaptable, and fulfilling environment where individuals and the collective thrive.

# Respect: The Cornerstone of Human Connection in Value-Centric Management (VCM P.I.P.E™)

In the intricate tapestry of Value-Centric Management (VCM P.I.P.E™), respect emerges as a foundational thread, weaving together individuals and fostering a culture of dignity, value, and collaboration. It's a philosophy that transcends hierarchical structures and power dynamics, recognizing the inherent worth of every person within the group.

**The Essence of Respect**

At its core, respect in VCM P.I.P.E™ is about acknowledging and valuing the unique contributions of each individual. It's about treating everyone with courtesy, consideration, and empathy, regardless of their position or title. It's about creating an environment where everyone feels heard, seen, and appreciated.

This approach challenges the traditional notion of respect as something reserved solely for those in positions of authority. In a VCM P.I.P.E™ environment, respect is a two-way street, flowing freely between leaders and followers, colleagues and peers. It's about recognizing that everyone has something valuable to offer, and that true success is achieved through mutual respect and collaboration.

**The Impact of Respect**

The impact of respect on an organization's culture and performance cannot be overstated. When individuals feel respected, they are more likely to be engaged, motivated, and committed to their work. They feel a sense of belonging and purpose, which translates into increased productivity, creativity, and innovation.

Moreover, respect fosters a sense of trust and psychological safety within the group. When people feel safe to express their opinions and ideas without fear of judgment or ridicule, it creates an environment where open communication and collaboration can thrive. This can lead to better decision-making, improved problem-solving, and a greater sense of collective ownership.

Furthermore, respect is a key ingredient in building strong and lasting relationships. When individuals feel valued and appreciated, they are more likely to develop a sense of loyalty and commitment to the group. This can lead to increased retention, reduced turnover, and a more cohesive and supportive work environment.

**Cultivating Respect**

Creating a culture of respect requires intentional effort and a commitment to modeling respectful behavior at all levels of the organization. It's about actively listening to others, acknowledging their perspectives, and valuing their contributions. It's about creating a safe space where individuals feel comfortable expressing their opinions and ideas without fear of judgment or reprisal.

Moreover, it's about recognizing and celebrating the diversity within the group. Each person brings a unique set of experiences, skills, and perspectives to the table, and these differences should be embraced and valued. By fostering an inclusive environment where everyone feels respected and appreciated, organizations can tap into the full potential of their workforce and achieve remarkable results.

**Conclusion**

In the grand tapestry of VCM P.I.P.E™, respect is the golden thread that binds individuals together, creating a culture of dignity, value, and collaboration. It's a philosophy that recognizes the inherent worth of every person and empowers them to contribute their best. By fostering a culture of respect, organizations can unlock the full potential of their people, leading to increased engagement, innovation, and sustainable success.

# Justice: The Bedrock of Trust and Fairness in Value-Centric Management (VCM P.I.P.E™)

In the realm of Value-Centric Management (VCM P.I.P.E™), the principle of Justice stands as a pillar of integrity and fairness, ensuring that rewards and consequences are distributed equitably based on merit, not on personal relationships, titles, or any other extraneous factors. It's a philosophy that recognizes the importance of creating a system where individuals trust that their efforts and contributions will be recognized and rewarded fairly, fostering a sense of accountability and motivation.

**The Essence of Justice**

At its core, Justice in VCM P.I.P.E™ is about creating a level playing field where everyone is judged based on their actions and contributions, not on their personal connections or social standing. It's about ensuring that rewards, such as promotions, bonuses, or recognition, are given to those who truly deserve them, based on their performance and the value they create for the organization. Similarly, consequences, such as disciplinary actions or performance improvement plans, should be administered fairly and consistently, based on objective criteria and evidence. And lastly, its about implementing forgiveness and grace and empathy as well.

This approach challenges the traditional notion of favoritism and bias, where rewards and punishments might be influenced by personal relationships or subjective opinions. In a VCM P.I.P.E™ environment, Justice is blind, ensuring that everyone is treated equally and fairly, regardless of their background or social standing.

**The Impact of Justice**

The impact of Justice on an organization's culture and performance is profound. When individuals trust that the system is fair and equitable, they are more likely to be engaged, motivated, and committed to their work. They know that their efforts will be recognized and rewarded, and that any shortcomings will be addressed fairly and constructively.

Moreover, Justice fosters a sense of accountability and responsibility. When individuals know that they will be held accountable for their actions, both positive and negative, it encourages them to take ownership of their work and strive for excellence. It also creates a culture of transparency and trust, where individuals feel comfortable raising concerns or reporting issues without fear of reprisal.

Furthermore, Justice plays a crucial role in attracting and retaining top talent. In a competitive job market, individuals are drawn to organizations that have a reputation for fairness and equity. They want to work in an environment where their contributions are valued and their hard work is rewarded, regardless of their background or personal connections.

**Cultivating Justice**

Creating a culture of Justice requires a commitment to transparency, objectivity, and consistency. It's about establishing clear performance metrics and expectations, and ensuring that rewards and consequences are administered fairly and impartially. It's also about creating a safe space where individuals feel comfortable raising concerns or reporting issues without fear of retaliation.

Moreover, it's about fostering a culture of open communication and feedback, where individuals feel empowered to speak up and share their perspectives. This allows for continuous improvement and ensures that any potential biases or inequities are addressed promptly and effectively.

**Conclusion**

In the grand scheme of VCM P.I.P.E™, Justice serves as the bedrock upon which trust, fairness, and accountability are built. It's a philosophy that recognizes the inherent dignity and worth of every individual and ensures that they are treated with respect and equity. By fostering a culture of Justice, organizations can create a more engaged, motivated, and productive workforce, ultimately leading to sustainable success and a thriving community.

# Traditions and Rituals: The Glue that Binds People in Value-Centric Management (VCM P.I.P.E™)

In the vibrant tapestry of Value-Centric Management (VCM P.I.P.E™), traditions and rituals emerge as the subtle yet powerful threads that weave together the fabric of a cohesive and thriving community – and its culture. They are the shared experiences, the recurring practices, and the symbolic gestures that create a sense of belonging, identity, and purpose within a group.

**The Essence of Traditions and Rituals**

At their core, traditions and rituals are about creating a sense of continuity and connection. They are the touchstones that remind us of our shared history, values, and aspirations. They provide a sense of stability and grounding in a world that is constantly changing and evolving.

In a VCM P.I.P.E™ environment, traditions and rituals are not just empty formalities; they are meaningful expressions of the group's culture and values. They can take many forms, from weekly team lunches and annual celebrations to simple gestures of recognition and appreciation. The key is that they are authentic, relevant, and resonate with the members of the group.

**The Power of Shared Experiences**

Traditions and rituals create a sense of shared experience and collective memory. They provide opportunities for individuals to connect with one another on a deeper level, fostering a sense of camaraderie and belonging. Whether it's celebrating a team victory, marking a milestone achievement, or simply sharing a meal together, these shared experiences create bonds that transcend individual differences and strengthen the fabric of the group.

Moreover, traditions and rituals provide a sense of continuity and stability. In a world that is constantly changing, they offer a sense of grounding and reassurance. They remind us of our shared history and values, providing a compass for navigating the challenges and uncertainties of the future.

**Fostering Traditions and Rituals**

Creating and maintaining traditions and rituals requires intentionality and commitment. It's about identifying those practices that resonate with the group's culture and values, and then incorporating them into the fabric of everyday life. It's also about being open to new ideas and evolving traditions as the group grows and changes.

Moreover, it's important to ensure that traditions and rituals are inclusive and accessible to all members of the group. They should be designed to foster a sense of belonging and connection, not exclusion or division.

**Conclusion**

In the grand symphony of VCM P.I.P.E™, traditions and rituals are the subtle harmonies that enrich the overall composition. They are the expressions of shared values, the reminders of collective history, and the glue that binds individuals together in a common purpose. By fostering a culture rich in traditions and rituals, organizations can create a sense of belonging, identity, and purpose that transcends individual differences and propels the group towards greater heights.

# Celebration: Fueling the Fire of Achievement in Value-Centric Management (VCM P.I.P.E™)

In the vibrant ecosystem of Value-Centric Management (VCM P.I.P.E™), celebration isn't just an afterthought or a frivolous indulgence; it's a strategic imperative that fuels the fire of achievement and propels individuals and groups towards greater heights. It's a philosophy that recognizes the power of positive reinforcement and the profound impact it can have on motivation, engagement, and overall performance.

**The Essence of Celebration**

At its core, celebration in VCM P.I.P.E™ is about acknowledging and honoring accomplishments, both big and small. It's about creating a culture where success is recognized, appreciated, and shared, fostering a sense of pride, camaraderie, and collective accomplishment.

This approach challenges the traditional notion of celebration as something reserved solely for major milestones or extraordinary achievements. In a VCM P.I.P.E™ environment, celebration is woven into the fabric of everyday life, recognizing the value of incremental progress and the cumulative impact of individual and collective efforts.

**The Power of Positive Reinforcement**

Celebration acts as a powerful form of positive reinforcement, reinforcing desired behaviors and motivating individuals to strive for excellence. When accomplishments are acknowledged and celebrated, it creates a sense of positive momentum, encouraging individuals to continue pushing their boundaries and reaching for new heights.

Moreover, celebration fosters a sense of belonging and shared purpose. When individuals see their contributions being recognized and appreciated, it reinforces their sense of value and connection to the group. This can lead to increased engagement, loyalty, and a greater willingness to go the extra mile for the collective good.

Furthermore, celebration creates a culture of positivity and optimism. When success is celebrated, it creates an atmosphere of possibility and encourages individuals to embrace challenges with confidence and enthusiasm. This can lead to increased creativity, innovation, and a greater willingness to take risks.

**Cultivating a Culture of Celebration**

Creating a culture of celebration requires intentionality and a commitment to recognizing and appreciating accomplishments at all levels of the organization. It's about creating opportunities for individuals to share their successes, both big and small, and to receive recognition and appreciation from their peers and leaders.

This might involve implementing formal recognition programs, such as employee of the month awards or team celebrations. It could also include more informal practices, such as verbal praise, handwritten notes, or simply taking the time to acknowledge a job well done.

**Conclusion**

In the grand tapestry of VCM P.I.P.E™, celebration is the vibrant thread that adds color, energy, and joy to the organizational landscape. It's a philosophy that recognizes the power of positive reinforcement and harnesses it to fuel the fire of achievement. By fostering a culture of celebration, organizations can create a more engaged, motivated, and fulfilled workforce, ultimately leading to greater success and a thriving community.

# Capital Stewardship: Nurturing the Seeds of Prosperity in Value-Centric Management (VCM P.I.P.E™)

In the intricate ecosystem of Value-Centric Management (VCM P.I.P.E™), the principle of Capital Stewardship emerges as a cornerstone of sustainable growth and prosperity. It's a philosophy that recognizes the critical role of capital – financial, human, and intellectual – in fueling the engine of value creation and exchange. Each group must take care of its resources if the group is going to be successful at whatever its goals are.

**The Essence of Capital Stewardship**

At its core, Capital Stewardship is about responsible and effective management of resources. It's about recognizing that capital is not an unlimited resource, but rather a precious asset that must be nurtured, protected, and deployed strategically to achieve long-term success.

In a VCM P.I.P.E™ environment, Capital Stewardship is not just about maximizing profits or minimizing costs; it's about creating sustainable value for all stakeholders. It's about investing in the future, fostering innovation, and ensuring that the organization has the resources it needs to thrive in the long run.

## The Role of Capital

Capital, in its various forms, plays a vital role in the VCM P.I.P.E™ framework. Financial capital provides the fuel for operations, investments, and growth. Human capital represents the skills, knowledge, and creativity of the individuals within the organization. Intellectual capital encompasses the intangible assets, such as patents, trademarks, and brand reputation, that contribute to the organization's competitive advantage.

Effective Capital Stewardship involves recognizing the interconnectedness of these different forms of capital and managing them in a way that maximizes their collective impact. It's about investing in the development of human capital, protecting and leveraging intellectual property, and deploying financial resources in a way that generates sustainable returns.

## The Importance of Responsible Management

Responsible management of capital is essential for long-term success in a VCM P.I.P.E™ environment. It's about making informed decisions that balance short-term gains with long-term sustainability. It's about avoiding wasteful spending, minimizing risk, and ensuring that resources are allocated in a way that maximizes value creation.

Moreover, Capital Stewardship involves a commitment to transparency and accountability. It's about being open and honest about the organization's financial performance, investment decisions, and use of resources. This fosters trust among stakeholders and ensures that everyone is aligned around the common goal of creating sustainable value.

**Conclusion**

In the grand tapestry of VCM P.I.P.E™, Capital Stewardship is the careful hand that tends to the garden, ensuring that the seeds of prosperity are nurtured and protected. It's a philosophy that recognizes the critical role of capital in fueling growth and innovation, and emphasizes the importance of responsible management for long-term success. By embracing Capital Stewardship, organizations can create a sustainable and thriving ecosystem where value is created, shared, and preserved for generations to come.

# Experimentation: Embracing the Unknown in Value-Centric Management (VCM P.I.P.E™)

In the ever-evolving landscape of Value-Centric Management (VCM P.I.P.E™), experimentation emerges as a vital tool for growth, innovation, and adaptation. It's a philosophy that encourages individuals and organizations to step outside their comfort zones, explore new ideas, and embrace the unknown in pursuit of creating greater value. Yes, systems are important. Yes, structure is important. But we need to allow room for experimentation and creativity. It should be more about values and less about structures. It should be more about results, and less about methods.

**The Essence of Experimentation**

At its core, experimentation is about curiosity, exploration, and a willingness to learn. It's about recognizing that the path to progress is often paved with trial and error, and that failure is not an endpoint but a stepping stone to success. In a VCM P.I.P.E™ environment, experimentation is not just tolerated; it's actively encouraged and celebrated.

This approach challenges the traditional aversion to risk and the fear of failure that often stifle innovation. In a VCM P.I.P.E™ environment, individuals are empowered to test new ideas, challenge assumptions, and push the boundaries of what's possible. It's about creating a culture where curiosity and exploration are rewarded, and where failure is seen as a valuable learning opportunity.

**The Role of Learning**

In a VCM P.I.P.E™ context, experimentation is intrinsically linked to learning. It's about adopting a growth mindset, where individuals are constantly seeking to expand their knowledge, skills, and capabilities. It's about embracing the unknown, recognizing that every experiment, whether successful or not, provides valuable insights that can inform future decisions and actions.

This approach fosters a culture of continuous improvement, where individuals and organizations are constantly evolving and adapting to meet the changing needs of the market and the world around them. It's about staying ahead of the curve, anticipating trends, and proactively seeking out new opportunities for value creation.

**Benefits of Experimentation**

Embracing experimentation can lead to numerous benefits for individuals and organizations. It fosters innovation, allowing for the development of new products, services, and business models that create greater value for customers and stakeholders. It enhances adaptability and resilience, enabling organizations to navigate the complexities of a rapidly changing world with agility and confidence.

Moreover, experimentation promotes a culture of learning and growth. When individuals are encouraged to experiment and take risks, they develop new skills, expand their knowledge, and build their confidence. This can lead to increased engagement, motivation, and a greater sense of ownership and responsibility.

**Fostering Experimentation**

Creating a culture of experimentation requires a deliberate and sustained effort. It's about providing individuals with the time, resources, and autonomy to explore new ideas and test their hypotheses. It's also about creating a safe space where failure is not stigmatized but rather seen as a natural part of the learning process.

Moreover, it's about celebrating both successes and failures, recognizing that every experiment, regardless of its outcome, contributes to the collective knowledge and growth of the group.

By fostering an environment where experimentation is encouraged and rewarded, organizations can unlock the full potential of their people and achieve remarkable results.

**Conclusion**

In the dynamic landscape of VCM P.I.P.E™, experimentation is the compass that guides us towards new horizons of value creation and innovation. It's a philosophy that embraces the unknown, celebrates learning, and empowers individuals to push the boundaries of what's possible. By fostering a culture of experimentation, organizations can navigate the complexities of the modern world with agility, resilience, and a relentless pursuit of progress.

# Vision: Illuminating the Path Forward in Value-Centric Management (VCM P.I.P.E™)

In the dynamic landscape of Value-Centric Management (VCM P.I.P.E™), a compelling vision serves as the guiding star, illuminating the path towards a brighter future. It's a philosophy that recognizes the profound impact of a shared aspiration, uniting individuals and organizations in a common purpose and providing a sense of direction and meaning.

**The Essence of Vision**

At its core, vision in VCM P.I.P.E™ is about painting a picture of a desired future state. It's about articulating a clear and compelling aspiration that resonates with the values and aspirations of the group. It's not just about setting goals or objectives; it's about creating a shared sense of purpose that inspires and motivates individuals to contribute their best.

This approach draws inspiration from the biblical proverb, "Where there is no vision, the people perish." It recognizes that without a clear sense of direction, individuals and organizations can become adrift, lacking the motivation and focus needed to achieve their full potential. A compelling vision, on the other hand, acts as a beacon, guiding actions and decisions and providing a sense of meaning and purpose.

**The Role of Vision in VCM P.I.P.E™**

In a VCM P.I.P.E™ environment, vision plays a crucial role in aligning individual and collective efforts. It provides a framework for decision-making, ensuring that actions and initiatives are consistent with the overarching goals and aspirations of the group. It also serves as a source of inspiration, motivating individuals to strive for excellence and contribute their unique talents to the realization of the shared vision.

Moreover, a compelling vision can act as a powerful magnet, attracting like-minded individuals and organizations who share the same values and aspirations. It can foster a sense of community and belonging, creating a powerful sense of collective purpose that transcends individual differences.

**Crafting a Compelling Vision**

Creating a compelling vision requires a deep understanding of the group's values, aspirations, and potential. It's about envisioning a future state that is both ambitious and achievable, inspiring yet grounded in reality. It's also about communicating that vision in a way that resonates with individuals, igniting their passion and commitment.

A well-crafted vision should be clear, concise, and easily understood. It should paint a vivid picture of the desired future state, highlighting the benefits and impact it will have on individuals, the organization, and the broader community. It should also be aspirational, challenging the group to reach beyond its current limitations and strive for greatness.

**Conclusion**

In the dynamic landscape of VCM P.I.P.E™, a compelling vision serves as the North Star, guiding individuals and organizations towards a brighter future. It's a philosophy that recognizes the power of shared aspiration and harnesses it to create a sense of purpose, motivation, and collective achievement. By crafting and communicating a clear and compelling vision, leaders can inspire their teams, attract like-minded individuals, and create a lasting legacy of value creation and positive impact.

# Authentic Data Transparency: Illuminating the Path to Collective Intelligence in Value-Centric Management (VCM P.I.P.E™)

In the intricate dance of Value-Centric Management (VCM P.I.P.E™), the principle of Authentic Data Transparency emerges as a guiding light, illuminating the path towards collective intelligence and informed decision-making. It's a philosophy that recognizes the power of shared knowledge and the transformative impact it can have on an organization's ability to adapt, innovate, and thrive.

**The Essence of Authentic Data Transparency**

At its core, Authentic Data Transparency is about fostering a culture of openness and information sharing. It's about recognizing that every individual within an organization possesses valuable data, insights, and perspectives that, when shared, can contribute to the collective intelligence of the group.

In a VCM P.I.P.E™ environment, data transparency is not just about making information available; it's about creating a culture where individuals feel empowered and encouraged to share their knowledge freely and openly. It's about breaking down silos, promoting cross-functional collaboration, and ensuring that everyone has access to the information they need to make informed decisions and contribute their best.

**The Power of Shared Knowledge**

The power of shared knowledge lies in its ability to amplify individual insights and create a more comprehensive understanding of the challenges and opportunities facing the organization. When data is transparently shared, it allows for a more holistic and nuanced perspective, enabling the group to identify patterns, trends, and potential solutions that might not be apparent to any single individual.

Moreover, Authentic Data Transparency fosters a sense of trust and collaboration. When individuals feel that they have access to the same information as their colleagues and leaders, it creates a sense of equity and shared responsibility. This can lead to increased engagement, motivation, and a greater willingness to contribute to the collective good.

## The Role of Continuous Learning

In a VCM P.I.P.E™ context, Authentic Data Transparency is intrinsically linked to the principle of continuous learning. As individuals gain new experiences and insights, they are encouraged to share their knowledge with the group, contributing to the ongoing evolution of the collective intelligence. This creates a dynamic and adaptive learning environment where the organization is constantly evolving and improving.

## Fostering Authentic Data Transparency

Creating a culture of Authentic Data Transparency requires a deliberate and sustained effort. It's about establishing clear channels for communication and information sharing, and ensuring that everyone has access to the data they need to perform their roles effectively. It's also about creating a safe space where individuals feel comfortable sharing their insights and perspectives without fear of judgment or reprisal.

Moreover, it's about recognizing and rewarding those who contribute to the collective knowledge base. When individuals see that their contributions are valued and appreciated, it reinforces the importance of sharing information and encourages continued participation.

**Conclusion**

In the grand tapestry of VCM P.I.P.E™, Authentic Data Transparency is the illuminating thread that connects individuals, ideas, and insights, creating a vibrant and interconnected network of shared knowledge. It's a philosophy that recognizes the power of collective intelligence and harnesses it to drive innovation, enhance decision-making, and ultimately achieve greater success. By fostering a culture of openness, trust, and continuous learning, organizations can tap into the full potential of their people and create a brighter future for all.

# Personal Connections and Team Building: Nurturing the Human Element in Value-Centric Management (VCM P.I.P.E™)

In the intricate framework of Value-Centric Management (VCM P.I.P.E™), this chapter on Personal Connections and Team Building emerges as a heartfelt reminder of the human element at the core of every successful endeavor. It's a philosophy that recognizes the profound impact of genuine relationships, mutual respect, and a shared sense of belonging on individual and collective well-being.

**The Essence of Personal Connections**

At its core, Personal Connections in VCM P.I.P.E™ is about fostering an environment where individuals feel seen, heard, and valued. It's about recognizing that each person brings a unique set of experiences, perspectives, and aspirations to the table, and that these differences should be celebrated and embraced – and converted into production centers, or sources of value creation.

This approach challenges the traditional notion of the workplace as a purely transactional space, where relationships are often secondary to tasks and objectives. In a VCM P.I.P.E™ environment, personal connections are not just encouraged; they are actively cultivated and nurtured, creating a sense of community and shared purpose.

**The Power of Team Building**

Team building in VCM P.I.P.E™ goes beyond icebreakers and trust falls. It's about creating opportunities for individuals to connect on a deeper level, to understand each other's strengths and weaknesses, and to build trust and mutual respect. It's about fostering a sense of camaraderie and shared responsibility, where everyone feels invested in the success of the group.

This approach recognizes that strong teams are built on a foundation of genuine relationships. When individuals feel connected to their colleagues and leaders, they are more likely to be engaged, motivated, and committed to their work. They are also more likely to collaborate effectively, share knowledge freely, and support each other through challenges.

**Nurturing the Human Element**

Nurturing the human element in a VCM P.I.P.E™ environment involves a multi-faceted approach. It's about creating opportunities for informal interactions, such as team lunches, social events, or simply taking the time to chat and connect with colleagues on a personal level. It's also about recognizing and celebrating individual achievements, fostering a culture of appreciation and gratitude.

Moreover, it's about creating a safe space where individuals feel comfortable expressing their thoughts and feelings, and where vulnerability is seen as a strength, not a weakness. This allows for deeper connections and a greater sense of empathy and understanding within the group.

**The Ripple Effect**

The impact of strong personal connections and effective team building extends far beyond individual well-being. It creates a positive ripple effect that permeates the entire organization, fostering a culture of collaboration, innovation, and shared success. When individuals feel connected to their colleagues and leaders, they are more likely to go the extra mile, take initiative, and contribute their unique talents to the collective good.

Moreover, a strong sense of community and belonging can lead to increased employee retention, reduced turnover, and a more positive organizational reputation. It can also attract top talent who are seeking a workplace where they feel valued, supported, and connected to a larger purpose.

**Conclusion**

In the grand tapestry of VCM P.I.P.E™, personal connections and team building are the vibrant threads that weave together the human element, creating a rich and fulfilling organizational experience. It's a philosophy that recognizes the power of genuine relationships and harnesses it to create a culture of collaboration, innovation, and shared success. By nurturing the human element, organizations can unlock the full potential of their people and achieve remarkable results.

# Customization: Tailoring VCM P.I.P.E™ for Unique Contexts in Value-Centric Management (VCM P.I.P.E™)

In the vibrant tapestry of human organizations, no two entities are exactly alike. Each possesses its own unique blend of personalities, cultures, goals, and challenges. Value-Centric Management (VCM P.I.P.E™) recognizes this inherent diversity and emphasizes the importance of customization, tailoring its principles to the specific context of each group.

**The Essence of Customization**

At its core, customization in VCM P.I.P.E™ is about recognizing that a one-size-fits-all approach rarely leads to optimal outcomes. It's about understanding the unique characteristics of each group and adapting the principles of VCM P.I.P.E™ to best suit their needs and aspirations.

This approach challenges the traditional notion of rigid frameworks and standardized solutions. In a VCM P.I.P.E™ environment, flexibility and adaptability are key. It's about recognizing that what works for one organization may not work for another, and that the true power of VCM P.I.P.E™ lies in its ability to be molded and shaped to fit the unique contours of each group.

**Embracing Diversity**

Customization in VCM P.I.P.E™ is also about embracing diversity. Every group, whether it's a business, a classroom, a community organization, or a sports team, has its own distinct culture, values, and goals. It's about recognizing and celebrating these differences, and tailoring the implementation of VCM P.I.P.E™ to leverage these unique strengths and address specific challenges.

This approach fosters a sense of ownership and empowerment, as individuals feel that the system is designed to support their specific needs and aspirations. It also promotes a sense of authenticity and alignment, ensuring that the principles of VCM P.I.P.E™ are integrated seamlessly into the fabric of the group's culture.

**The Art of Adaptation**

Customization in VCM P.I.P.E™ is an ongoing process of learning, adaptation, and refinement. It's about constantly evaluating the effectiveness of the implemented principles and making adjustments as needed. It's also about being open to new ideas and approaches, and incorporating them into the framework in a way that enhances value creation and fosters collective well-being.

This requires a willingness to experiment, to learn from both successes and failures, and to continuously evolve the implementation of VCM P.I.P.E™ to meet the changing needs of the group. It's about creating a dynamic and adaptive system that supports growth, innovation, and sustainable success.

**Conclusion**

In the vibrant tapestry of human organizations, customization is the brushstroke that adds depth, nuance, and individuality to the canvas of VCM P.I.P.E™. It's a philosophy that recognizes the inherent diversity of groups and empowers them to tailor the principles to their unique contexts. By embracing customization, organizations can unlock the full potential of VCM P.I.P.E™, creating a thriving ecosystem where individuals and the collective flourish.

# Conclusion: Embracing Value-Centric Management (VCM P.I.P.E™) for a Thriving Future

The chapters we've explored together paint a vivid picture of Value-Centric Management (VCM P.I.P.E™), a philosophy that transcends traditional management paradigms and places the creation and exchange of value at the heart of human interaction. From equity and leadership to collaboration and celebration, VCM P.I.P.E™ offers a holistic approach to fostering a thriving and fulfilling environment for individuals and organizations alike.

By embracing the principles of VCM P.I.P.E™, organizations, companies, classrooms, and groups of all kinds can unlock their full potential and achieve remarkable results. They can create a culture of innovation, collaboration, and continuous improvement, where individuals feel empowered to contribute their unique talents and perspectives. They can foster a sense of shared purpose and collective responsibility, where everyone is invested in the success of the group.

But the impact of VCM P.I.P.E™ extends far beyond individual organizations. Imagine a world where every entity, from small businesses to multinational corporations, from local schools to global institutions, embraces the principles of value creation and exchange. It's a world where collaboration triumphs over competition, where innovation flourishes, and where individuals are empowered to reach their full potential.

In such a world, we would see a dramatic shift in the way we work, learn, and interact with one another. We would see a greater emphasis on collaboration, creativity, and continuous learning. We would see a more equitable distribution of resources and opportunities, where everyone has a chance to contribute and thrive.

Moreover, we would witness a more sustainable and prosperous economy, where organizations are driven not just by profit but by a genuine desire to create value for all stakeholders. We would see a reduction in waste, a greater focus on social and environmental responsibility, and a more equitable distribution of wealth and opportunity.

In essence, VCM P.I.P.E™ offers a blueprint for a better future, a future where individuals and organizations are aligned around a shared purpose of creating and exchanging value. It's a future where collaboration, innovation, and sustainable growth are not just ideals but lived realities.

The journey towards this future begins with a single step. It begins with a commitment to embrace the principles of VCM P.I.P.E™ and to integrate them into the very fabric of our organizations and communities. It's a journey that requires courage, creativity, and a willingness to challenge the status quo. But the rewards are immeasurable, both for individuals and for the collective.

So let us embark on this journey together, with a shared vision of a world where value creation and exchange are at the heart of human interaction. Let us build a future where everyone has the opportunity to thrive, where organizations are driven by a sense of purpose, and where the collective good is always paramount. The path forward is clear, and the time to act is now.